Frida Kahlo

Frida Kahlo
An Illustrated Life

María Hesse

Translated by Achy Obejas

University of Texas Press ♠ Austin

First edition: October 2016
© 2016, María Hesse
© 2016, for the Spanish-language edition throughout the world:
Penguin Random House Grupo Editorial, S.A.U.
Travessera de Gràcia, 47–49.08021 Barcelona
First University of Texas Press edition, 2018
English-language translation © 2018, Achy Obejas
All rights reserved
Printed in China by Four Colour Print Group

Requests for permission to reproduce material from
this work should be sent to:
Permissions
University of Texas Press
P.O. Box 7819
Austin, TX 78713–7819
utpress.utexas.edu/rp-form

∞ The paper used in this book meets the minimum requirements of
ANSI/NISO Z39.48–1992 (R1997) (Permanence of Paper).

Library of Congress Cataloging-in-Publication Data

Names: Hesse, María, author. | Obejas, Achy, 1956–, translator.
Title: Frida Kahlo : an illustrated life / María Hesse ; translation by Achy
Obejas.
Other titles: Frida Kahlo. English
Description: First University of Texas Press edition. | Austin : University of
Texas Press, 2018. | Originally published in Spanish as "Frida Kahlo: una
biografía" by Penguin Random House Grupe Editorial in 2016. | Includes
bibliographical references.
Identifiers: LCCN 2018003957
        ISBN 978-1-4773-1728-0 (cloth : alk. paper)
        ISBN 978-1-4773-1729-7 (library e-book)
        ISBN 978-1-4773-1730-3 (nonlibrary e-book)
Subjects: LCSH: Kahlo, Frida. | Women painters—Mexico—Biography. |
Painters—Mexico—Biography.
Classification: LCC ND259.K33 .H47513 2018 | DDC 759.972 [B] —dc23
LC record available at https://lccn.loc.gov/2018003957

doi:10.7560/317280

For Alfonso: You make me
a better person.

To build a wall around your
suffering is to risk that it'll eat
you up from the inside out.
— Frida Kahlo

Contents

Introduction

When so much has been written about Frida Kahlo, why do it again?

It seems we all know Frida Kahlo. Well, at the very least, we all have a more or less definite image of her character and of her as an artist. She left us an ample record of her life through interviews, letters, her diary, and obviously, her work. But no matter how much we know, no matter how much we read, no matter how much we study her art, it always feels as if we know only part of her life and of what was on her mind.

Frida embellished her stories, Frida invented, Frida told the truth, Frida contradicted herself. She would change her version of a story from letter to letter, according to the urgency of the moment in which she found herself. Always living in extremes, going from color to black, from happiness to the most profound sadness, she'd go from laughing and singing and loving how she attracted attention to the silence and loneliness of her studio, where she painted from a place of absolute anguish. But that's not important because that is the source of Frida's charm and magic. The exact way things happened isn't important. What is really interesting is how she felt, and we can certainly garner an idea of that.

This book isn't about Frida's real life or even the one she invented. It is a blend of the two because I think some aspects of her real life were more interesting than her fiction, but at other times I would rather respect the truth of the life she wanted to tell us.

That said, all that's left is for me to offer a bit of advice: If you want to know the most authentic aspects of her life, immerse yourself in her paintings, in which she left us brief messages about who she was. It is in her paintings where the real Frida lives.

Frida Kahlo

I paint myself because I'm what I know best. I never paint dreams or nightmares; I paint my own reality.

My name is Magdalena Carmen Frida Kahlo y Calderón, and I was born July 6, 1907, in Coyoacán. Since birth, I've had to struggle with a medical condition I've had all my life. Some say I had polio, but in fact I had spina bifida.

1925

Life insists on being my friend and destiny my enemy.

On September 17, the bus I was riding in crashed into a streetcar. I was injured, on the verge of death.

1929

I wish I could give you what you've never had, but even then you wouldn't know how marvelous it is to love you.

On August 21, I married Diego Rivera.

1931—1934

We have to be honest, we women can't live without pain.

Diego and I moved to the United States. I had a miscarriage. I missed Mexico so much.

1935

The only good thing is that I've started to get used to suffering.

We come back to Mexico. Diego has an affair with my sister.

1937

Man is master of his destiny and his destiny is the earth, but he destroys it and is left with no destiny.

During his exile, we take in Trotsky. Inevitably, I have a romance with him.

1939

They thought I was a surrealist.

I exhibit in Paris. The French give me a great welcome.

1939

I've had two grave accidents in my life: the one in which a bus threw me down to the ground . . . The other is Diego.

Diego asks me for a divorce.

1940

I drank to drown my sorrows, but those wretches learned to swim.

I was interrogated after Trotsky's assassination. I'm in ill health and my sadness deepens. After a few months of separation, Diego and I are getting married again.

1947—1952

Feet, why do I need you, since I have wings to fly?

My adventure with innumerable surgeries begins. In 1952 they amputate my right leg.

1953

Doc, if you let me drink this tequila, I promise I won't drink at my funeral.

My first show in Mexico comes together. The doctor won't let me get out of bed. Complying with his orders, I'm carried to my opening in my bed.

1954

I hope the exit is joyous, and I hope to never come back.

I'm barely forty-seven years old, but my body is already exhausted from so much pain. All suffering has an end.

She plays alone

My name is Magdalena Carmen Frida Kahlo y Calderón. I was born July 6, 1907, in Coyoacán, but I always liked to say I was born in 1910 instead, not because of the frivolity of making myself seem younger but because that's the year of the Mexican Revolution, and I'm revolution.

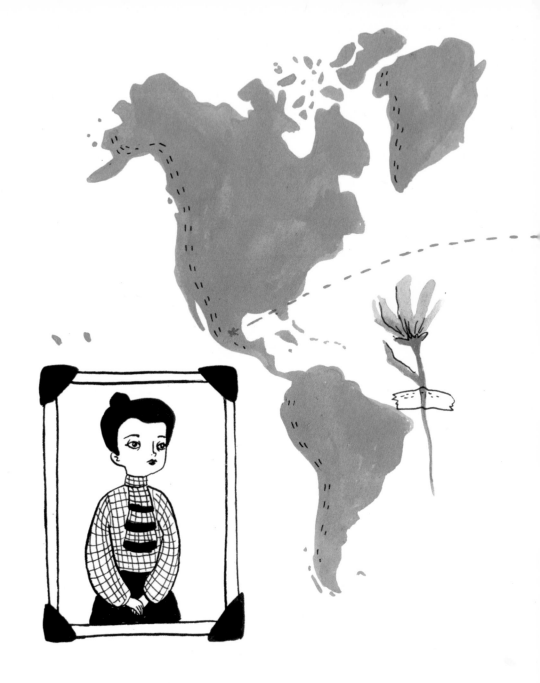

My mother was a woman of short stature, with very pretty eyes, a very elegant mouth, and bronze skin. She was a belle of Oaxaca. Very likable, active, intelligent. She didn't know how to read or write, only how to count money.

My father, Guillermo Kahlo, was an interesting man who moved with grace. He was serene, hardworking, and brave. He was intelligent and refined, brave because he suffered from epilepsy for many years, but it never kept him from attending to his work.

Guillermo Kahlo emigrated from Germany to Mexico when he was eighteen years old. He married María Cardeño Espino, and for a while, he worked at a jewelry store where he met Matilde Calderón, my mother.

My father's first wife died in childbirth with their second daughter.

Three months later—on February 21, 1898—he married Matilde, and on August 21 of that same year the first of my sisters was born.

When they got married, he began to work as a photographer, like my maternal grandfather, and he built La Casa Azul. He loved my mother deeply, yet she was never truly happy with him because she couldn't forget her first love, also German, who had committed suicide.

Matilde

Me

I was the third of four sisters. Cristina, my younger sister, was born only eleven months after me. We were always great friends.

The two daughters my father had with his first wife were sent off to boarding school shortly after he married again, so I barely had contact with them.

When I was seven, I helped Matilde, who was fifteen, run away to Veracruz with her boyfriend. Matita was my mother's favorite, and when she left, my mother became hysterical . . . When Mati left, my father did not say a word.

We didn't see her again until four years later.

Cristina   Adriana

When I was a little girl, I'd breathe on the window of what was then my room and use my finger to draw a door. In my imagination, I'd go through that door with great joy and urgency.

I would cross the plain until I got to a dairy called PINZÓN. I'd jump inside through the Ó in PINZÓN and quickly go down below the ground, where my imaginary friend always waited for me.

She was very cheerful and would laugh and laugh soundlessly. I don't remember her face. She was agile and danced as if she weighed nothing at all. I followed all her moves as she danced and told her all my real problems. What problems? I don't remember.

PINZÓN

The Mexican Revolution broke out in 1910, and the government of dictator Porfirio Díaz fell. The struggle continued for more than ten years. My mother supported the Zapatistas. She fed them and cured their wounds while Cristina and I hid wherever we could.

The people rose up, a great creative movement came into being, and the country lived through years of transformation.

During 1914, all we heard was the whistling of bullets. I still remember that extraordinary sound. Hidden in a grand dresser that smelled like walnuts, Cristi and I would count the bullets as our parents kept watch so we wouldn't fall into the hands of the guerrillas.

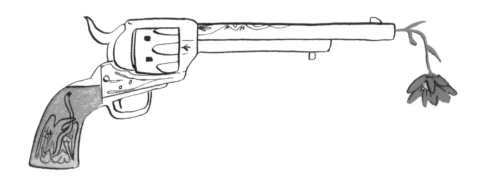

They say I contracted polio when I was six and that this was the reason my right leg was atrophied. But that wasn't the reason. My mother had a folic acid deficiency during the pregnancies following my sister Matilde. That lack meant the children who came later were born with spina bifida. As a result, I had severe scoliosis, and my right leg was weaker, shorter, and thinner than my left. The kids would call me "Frida Kahlo Pegleg Hollow."

I was three years old before I learned to walk without help. In order to avoid being talked about and so the difference between my sister and me—we were only eleven months apart—wouldn't reveal my delay, they kept us home all that time. Cristina also had to undergo a series of surgeries on her back and had to wear a corset her entire life.

They decided to say I had had polio instead so as to not diminish my marital prospects, because back then it wasn't known whether spina bifida was hereditary or contagious. This doubt haunted me all my life, and I wondered if I could bring a healthy baby into the world.

When I could finally walk alone, my parents sent my sister and me to school. They decided to lie about our ages, making us three years younger than we actually were; this was so we wouldn't seem so far behind the other students in our class. I've kept the fictitious birth date ever since because it coincides with the Mexican Revolution.

My father helped me overcome my condition with a rather unconventional rehab program for a little girl in those days: I swam, I fought, and I boxed.

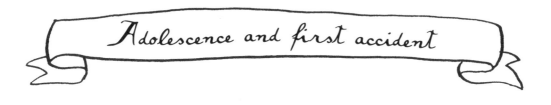

Adolescence and first accident

I was always my father's favorite. He said I was the most intelligent of his daughters and the one most like him. After several fights with my mother, he managed to let me take the entrance exam for the National Preparatory School. Of two thousand students, I was one of the thirty-five women admitted. I was very interested in anatomy and dreamt of being a doctor.

At school I became a member of Los Cachuchas. We identified with socialist and nationalist ideas, and we reclaimed Mexico's indigenous past. Alejandro Gómez Arias, Miguel N. Lara, José Zález Ramírez, Alfonso Villa, Agustín Lira, Carmen Jaime. We found ourselves at the dawn of a new nation, and we had the opportunity to participate in shaping it.

Alejandro, my good friend, was a member of Los Cachuchas, and, without realizing it, I fell in love with him.

In those days, I was overcome by passion for everything around me.

I loved to ride to school on rented bikes I often forgot to return.

I used to fill my backpack with treasures to accompany my books. Small rocks, dried butterflies, and little notebooks I'd make myself.

It was a decisive time in my life. My mother worried I'd end up becoming an atheist, and my childhood friends began to keep their distance, fearing I'd lost my reputation by rejecting the stereotypical behavior expected of women. But none of that mattered to me, and I told Alejandro:

I don't care. I like how I am.

In those days, young women had to act and dress in a way with which I didn't identify and which made me uncomfortable. I couldn't be myself, and what I wanted was to do what I wanted to do. Later, Alejandro said that, for me, "sex was a way of enjoying life, a kind of vital impulse."

A rumor went around that I had a romance with a woman librarian.

Soon, I stopped going to classes. I was much more interested in people. Luckily, I loved to read and to learn on my own, so I never had any problems when it came to grades on my exams.

The economic situation in our home worsened so that eventually we had to mortgage the house and sell most of the furniture and decorations. I decided to get a job to help my family.

In 1922 I met the great painter Diego Rivera. Diego had been chosen to paint a mural in the Bolívar Amphitheater at the National Preparatory School. I devoted myself to bothering him during his time there in order to get his attention. I'd wax the floor so he'd slip, I'd steal his food. In fact, whenever I saw him flirting with the model posing for him, I'd scare him by shouting a warning that his wife was coming.

One afternoon I asked him if I could stay a while
to watch him work. Time passed without my realizing it.
I was completely entranced for more than three hours. That's
the day I knew Diego Rivera would be the father of my children.

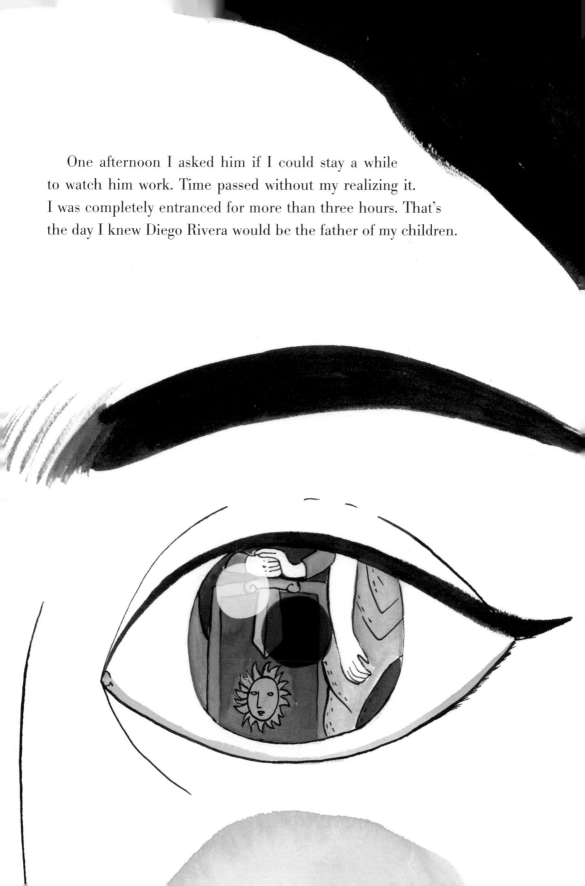

In 1925 I had my first accident.

I climbed on the bus with Alejandro Gómez Arias. Moments later, the bus crashed into a train on the Xochimilco line. It was a strange collision; it wasn't violent but silent, in a kind of slow motion. Everyone was hurt. Me, more than anyone.

We had taken another bus before this one. But I'd lost a little umbrella, and we got off to look for it. That's why we got on that bus, the one that destroyed me.

It's a lie that you're aware of the crash. A lie too, about crying. I shed no tears. The impact hurled us forward, and the handrail went through me the way a sword lances a bull.

On the ground, I was strangely nude and covered in blood and the gold dust a worker had been carrying. The people around me cried, "Help the little dancer!"

I was taken to the Red Cross Hospital. The doctors thought I wouldn't live. I didn't think so, either.

My oldest sister, Matilde, read about the accident in the newspapers and was the first to come be with me. She didn't leave my side for three months; she was with me day and night. My mother was rendered mute for a month by the shock of it all and didn't go see me. When my sister Adriana found out, she fainted. The news caused my father such sadness that he became ill and couldn't come see me for twenty days.

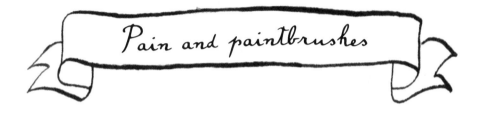
Pain and paintbrushes

How many days was I confined to bed? If I add them all up, they come out to more than a year.

Fractures in my third and fourth lumbar vertebrae, three fractures in my pelvis, eleven fractures in my right foot, dislocation of my

left elbow, a serious wound in my abdomen pro-
duced by a steel bar that tore my left labia.
Acute peritonitis. Such cystitis that I needed an
IV for several days.

I said the bar on the bus perforated my uterus to justify the loss of my virginity, but the bar really came out much higher than that, at about the height of my pelvic bone.

For a long time, in spite of the doctors' prognosis, I wanted to believe it was the accident that was responsible for my inability to have children.

In order to heal, I had to spend long days in bed and wear many different plaster casts, each one worse than the other. I had to learn that pain would be with me for the rest of my life.

My mother had an idea to lift my spirits. She wanted to turn my bed into a refuge. She had a canopy built above it with a mirror in it. My father gave me paints. I began to do self-portraits because I was spending so much time alone and because I'm the subject I know best.

Without really thinking about it, I began to paint. Nothing seemed more natural than to paint what was out of my reach.

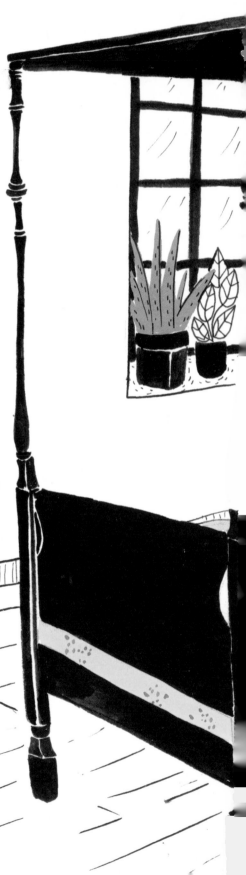

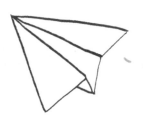

Alejandro left for Europe. I tried desperately not to lose him and wrote him letters for a very long time. But little by little, my love for him evaporated, and I got tired of waiting for him. A part of me had died and I was no longer the same person, so being together didn't make sense anymore.

Why do you study so much? What secrets are you looking for? Life will reveal everything soon enough. I already know everything, even without reading or writing. Not long ago, just a matter of days, I was a little girl and walked through a world of color, of solid and tangible things. Everything was mysterious and things were obscured. I liked to figure things out, to learn, more than to play. If you only knew how terrible it is to suddenly know everything, as if a bolt of lightning had illuminated the world. I now inhabit a painful planet, as transparent as ice, with nothing hidden, as if I had learned everything in seconds. My friends, my classmates, have slowly become women. I matured in an instant, and today everything is white and lucid. I know there's nothing obscured. If there were, I would see it.

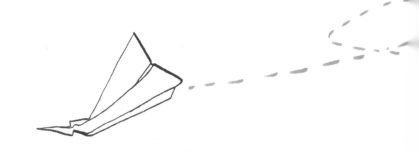

The elephant and the dove

Times heals (almost) all wounds. I began to hang out with groups of communists, Marxists, and political exiles. That's how I met Julio Antonio Mella, a Cuban revolutionary and communist exile, a contributor to *El Machete* magazine, and the lover of one of my best friends, the photographer Tina Modotti.

I recovered my passion for conversation, my joy in dancing and drinking tequila. At a party at Tina's, I saw Diego Rivera again. By that time, he was one of Mexico's most important painters.

He had been married to Lupe Marín, with whom he'd had two daughters. He had another daughter from a previous relationship with the Russian painter Marevna, and I knew he liked to collect lovers. I admired him, so I decided to show him my work and get his opinion.

I took four small pieces over to him while he was working up on a scaffold at the Department of Education. "Diego, come down," I called to him. And just like that, quite humbly, so kindly, he did.

"Look, I didn't come here to flirt with you or anything like that; I know you're a womanizer. I just came to show you my paintings. If they interest you, tell me; if they don't interest you, tell me just the same, so I can find something else to work on to help my parents." Then he said, "Look, in the first place, I'm very interested in your paintings, especially this self-portrait here, which is the most original. The other three seem to be influenced by things you've seen. Go home, paint something, and next Sunday I'll come by and let you know what I think." So that's what I did. "You have talent," he said.

We became friends, comrades, lovers. I called him paunchy and told him he had a frog face, and far from getting mad, he'd laugh and laugh and laugh.

I fell in love with Diego, and that displeased my parents because Diego was a communist and, according to them, he looked like a very fat Brueghel. They said it would be a wedding between an elephant and a dove. Nonetheless, I made all the arrangements at the Coyoacán registry so we could be married August 21, 1929. I borrowed skirts from my housemaid. She also lent me a blouse and a rebozo. I fit my foot into a boot with a brace, so it wouldn't be so noticeable, and we got married.

My father said to Diego, "Don't forget that my daughter is ill, and will be ill all her life. She's intelligent but not pretty. Think about it . . . If, in spite of everything, you still want to marry her, I will give my consent."

We had the celebration on the roof at Tina's house. Lupe got drunk and wanted to humiliate me. She came up to me, raised my skirt, and started shouting in front of everyone, "See those sticks? Those are the legs Diego prefers over mine." She let me go and left the house.

Diego was so drunk he did absolutely nothing. I was crying and very sad and went back to my house. A few days went by before he came to get me to take me to his house.

This dress is worn by the women of the Isthmus of Tehuantepec, where matriarchal traditions endure.

There was a time when I dressed like a boy, with short hair, pants, boots, and a leather coat. But when I went to see Diego, I wore my Tehuana dress.

By wearing long dresses, I could
hide my disabled right leg.

I usually wore a little bell
on my orthopedic boot.

Some time after I married Diego, Lupe went with me to buy things for the kitchen and taught me how to cook.

She also taught me how to prepare Diego's food so I could take it to him while he worked. We would pack it in baskets decorated with flowers and napkins embroidered with sayings.

To show my gratitude, I painted her portrait and gave it to her.

Ingredients

1 chicken, chopped
2 ¼ pounds ripe tomatoes
6 guajillo chiles
6 dried ancho chiles
2 onions
6 garlic cloves
1 cube of chicken bouillon
1 teaspoon cloves
1 teaspoon Jamaica pepper
½ cup sesame seeds
2 ¼ pounds of potatoes
1 bay leaf
⅝ cup of bitter chocolate
1 teaspoon oregano and chopped cilantro
1 cinnamon stick
Salt and pepper

Preparation

To make a red mole, cook the chicken with one onion, cilantro, the bay leaf, salt, and pepper on low heat until the meat is tender. Remove the chicken and set it aside.

Remove the seeds from the chiles and roast the chiles. Put them in boiling water and let them sit for twenty-five minutes.

Sauté the onion and garlic, then add the tomatoes, pepper, sesame seeds, chiles, cloves, broth, and chocolate. Blend it to a purée consistency.

While the sauce is cooking, add the potatoes, cinnamon stick, and spices. When the potatoes are tender, add the chicken.

Serve with boiled rice.

A little bit after the wedding, Diego was expelled from the Communist Party, but even though he couldn't continue to commune with his ideology, he still defended communism in his lectures and his work.

During that time, I was barely painting. I loved my life with Diego and being at home. I would take care of domestic chores and wait impatiently for his return. Every now and again I would take the food basket to him wherever he was working, just like Lupe had taught me.

But soon there was sadness. In less than a year, Diego began to cheat on me. He explained himself by telling me a doctor had told him he was incapable of monogamy. The anguish became unbearable when I had to have an abortion and to learn to live with the hopelessness of not having children.

I would cry inconsolably, then distract myself with cooking, cleaning, and sometimes painting. The feeling that my body carries within it all the world's wounds never, ever left me again.

In spite of everything, I loved him. I liked to go places with Diego, and I enjoyed watching him paint those majestic murals. Besides, he always asked my opinion about what he was doing and made me feel important.

Between one thing and another, I'd paint to pass the time. He painted for the people. I painted for myself.

Things I Loved

Every tick-tock is a second of life that goes by, flees, and never comes back. And there's so much intensity, so much curiosity, that the only problem is how to live it. May each one work things out as best they can.

collecting popular Mexican crafts and small objects

drinking

smoking

collecting jewelry

animals

going to the theater

listening to mariachis

collecting dolls

writing letters

singing, dancing, and having a grand time

CARMEN RIVERA
PINTÓ: SU RE-
TRATO EL
AÑO 1931

Gringolandia

In 1930 we moved to the United States. Diego had been commissioned to paint murals at the San Francisco Stock Exchange and the California School of Fine Arts.

In 1931 we were very excited and hopeful when we moved to New York because Diego had received an extraordinary honor: a solo show at MoMA.

I missed Mexico, but I was fascinated by that city. I loved the movies, especially Chaplin, the Marx Brothers, and Disney.

In those days, we stayed at luxury hotels and went from party to party. I'd walk in shouting, cursing and rude, because I loved to see the expressions on the faces of all those priggish people. I attracted a lot of attention, but in spite of the criticisms, I knew everyone adored me.

I was lucky to meet Lucienne Bloch while we lived there. She assisted Diego in the studio and would become one of my good friends.

In 1932 we moved to Detroit because Diego received a proposal to paint a mural for Henry Ford. Once in the city, I got pregnant again. It had barely been a year since the doctors had recommended I terminate my previous pregnancy.

Diego wasn't interested in having more children, but he told me to do whatever I wanted, and I decided to go ahead with the pregnancy. It was a terrible time. I felt lost, and to top it off, I was forced to rest because of the constant bleeding.

I got bored from having to stay home, so I took up painting again. It was the only thing that gave me comfort.

This time the doctor told me that, in his opinion, it was better to go to term than to end my pregnancy because, in spite of my bad physical state, I could have the baby without difficulty by cesarean.

On the fourth of July, during a sweltering summer night, I lost the baby and almost died. I spent thirty anguished days in the hospital, crying endlessly and bleeding. I was inconsolable and pleaded to see my baby, but they couldn't show it to me because it had never taken shape. While there, I drew, painted, and scribbled out my misery. "No woman had ever created more agonized poetry on canvas than Frida did in Detroit," Diego wrote about my paintings from those days.

On September 3 of that same year, I received a telegram telling me my mother had breast cancer and was gravely ill.

I left for Mexico the next day, accompanied by Lucienne.

The train ride was never-ending. I hemorrhaged again, and blood mixed with my tears.

On September 15, just a few days after we arrived at my parents' house, my mother died. My father was devastated, and the weight of his heartbreak made my return to the United States even more difficult. I wanted to stay in my country, but I longed to be by my Diego.

During this painful period, I became inspired by Mexican votives.

Traditionally, each town had an artist who specialized in these types of paintings to whom the people would go when they were overwhelmed with adversity. They would ask the artist to paint their tragedy. First, they would tell their story, and then they would choose the virgin or saint to whom they wanted to dedicate the offering. At the bottom, there would be an inscription that narrated what was happening in the painting.

When the painting was ready, they would pay the artist and take the painting to church to make an offering to the divinity and forget their torment.

For me, painting what happened to me was a way to leave my suffering behind and continue living and celebrating life.

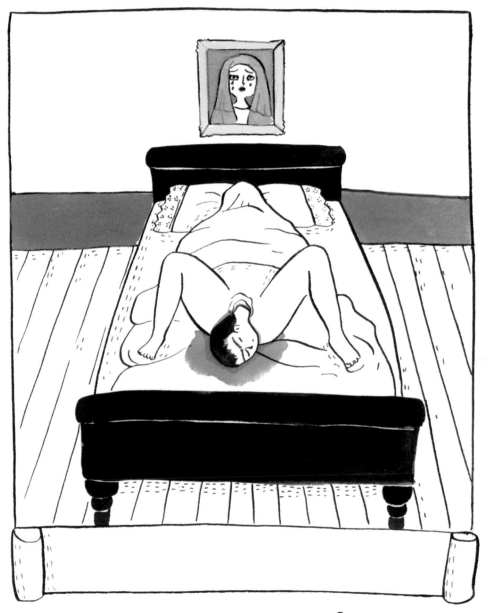

There was so much pain inside that I didn't know what to write.

Diego was deep into his work at Rockefeller Center. He had added in Lenin's face, which was considered a distasteful provocation. He refused to remove it, so, finally, he wasn't allowed to finish the work and the mural was destroyed.

As time went by, Diego had fewer and fewer commissions, and I missed Mexico terribly.

High society here drives me batty and all these rich guys enrage me, because I see thousands of people in the worst conditions, without so much as a crumb to eat or a place to sleep. This is what has most stayed with me. How terrible it is to see all these rich people partying day and night while thousands and thousands of people are dying of hunger.

After many fights, we went back home.

My second accident

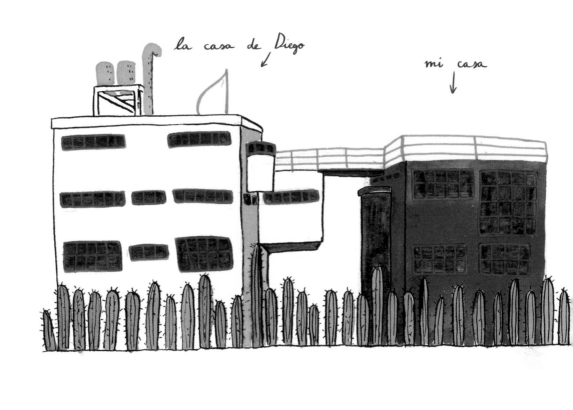

la casa de Diego

mi casa

When we came back to Mexico, we moved into the house on San Ángel. It had a very peculiar design: two independent houses connected by a narrow bridge. Like our love.

Diego was weak, thin, jaundiced, and spiritually broken. If he wasn't happy, I couldn't have peace of mind, and his health worried me more than my own. He thought everything happening to him was my fault because I had pressured him to return to Mexico.

When we came back, I was sick almost all of 1932. I had all five toes on my right foot amputated, and I again suffered a miscarriage. Diego cursed about our medical expenses and constantly blamed me for the economic ruin in which we were living.

But there was still an even greater sorrow for me to bear. Diego had begun a relationship with my sister Cristina.

I had never suffered so much and never imag-
ined I could feel such pain. She was the sister I
loved the most, and she meant so much to me in so
many ways. He lived a full life, without the stu-
pid emptiness of mine, but I never thought he'd be
everything to me and that I'd be nothing more than
a piece of junk to him. I realized I was just a girl
who'd been deceived and abandoned by a man she loved.

I suffered two grave accidents in my life: one in which a bus threw me to the ground . . .
The other is Diego.

Hurt, mistreated, and in anguish, I moved to a small apartment and cut my hair.

My situation struck me as ridiculous. I had wasted my best years doing nothing and being supported by a man, though I had been there to help him and for his benefit. After six years, his response was that fidelity is a bourgeois virtue and that it exists only to exploit people and for economic gain.

I went to New York for a brief visit, to forget. But all it did was prove I couldn't live far from Diego. So I came back, but on one condition: we would continue to be married, but we would lead independent lives. I began to have lovers, both men and women, but I was discreet because Diego was terribly jealous. One time he caught me with a Japanese sculptor, Isamu Noguchi, who had to run up on the roof because Diego burst in with a gun in his hand.

Some of my loves

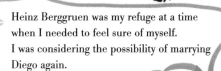

Heinz Berggruen was my refuge at a time when I needed to feel sure of myself. I was considering the possibility of marrying Diego again.

Alejandro Gómez Arias was my first love. After the accident on the bus, the relationship ended.

I won't be your girlfriend, but I'll always talk to you, even if you are incredibly rude to me.

Leo Eloesser was one of my surgeons in San Francisco.

It's so good for me to know you love me and that no matter where you are, you watch over me.

Nickolas Muray and I had a ten-year relationship. He was the person who understood me best. Our breakup was the most painful of all.

My beloved, my baby, and my lover.

Leon Trotsky, whom we took in during his exile, and I had a brief romance. We thought about the same things and wanted the world to be the way we dreamt it.

Chavela Vargas stayed at my house for a year. Did we really have an affair?

An extraordinary lesbian, and more, she became an erotic obsession. I don't know if she felt the same way.

In the
United States, I met
the Spaniard Josep Bartolí, a republican,
who had managed to escape from the Gestapo.

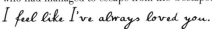
I feel like I've always loved you.

Jaqueline Lamba, André Breton's wife, with
whom he fled from the Nazis in France.

Then came new days with you.
Today, I wish my light could
touch you.

The sculptor Isamu Noguchi was invited by
Diego himself to do a public project at the
Abelardo L. Rodriguez market.
    Diego caught us in bed and Noguchi
    had to flee at gunpoint.

Diego, my father, my son, my universe.
Though I may have told
others I loved them and though
I may have had trysts and
kissed them, deep down I've
loved only YOU.

In the last years of my life, the majority of my
lovers were women.

Leon Trotsky

Midway through the 1930s, General Lázaro Cárdenas was elected president and communism swept into the capital. In 1936, civil war broke out in Spain, and together with others, we formed a solidarity committee to offer whatever support we could to the republicans fighting against fascism. That same year, Mexico offered political asylum to Leon Trotsky and Natalia Sedova, who had been expelled by Stalin from the Soviet Union after Lenin's death. They were being persecuted and had been condemned to death.

After much insisting by Diego, we took them in at La Casa Azul for a long time, with constant surveillance day and night.

I communicated with Trotsky in English so his wife couldn't understand us. We spent a lot of time together and slowly became more intimate until we began a brief relationship. I called him "love." We had a secret correspondence. But Natalia realized what was going on, and they decided to separate for a while. The distance between them didn't last long because he was as tied to his wife as I was to my Diego.

Leon asked me for our letters back and burned them so there would be no trace of what had happened between us.

A little later, while I was away, Diego and Trotsky had a fight. I don't know if it was over political differences or because my husband found out about our amorous relationship. In a short bit, they moved out of La Casa Azul. According to Diego, my husband, they weren't paying rent.

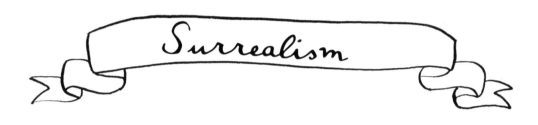

One day, André Breton, known in France as the father of surrealism, noticed my paintings and told me they were surrealist.

They thought I was a surrealist, but I wasn't. I've never painted dreams. I painted my own reality.

Around that time, Diego showed my work to Edward G. Robinson, the actor. He liked them so much he bought four for two hundred dollars each. I thought I could finally travel and do what I wanted without having to ask my husband for money.

Julien Levy invited me to do a show in his New York gallery, so I went back, this time without Diego.

I began to live my own life and to be recognized for my work, out from under my husband's shadow. The show went well and half the paintings were sold. I felt confident and seductive. I flirted with everyone, but the most important man in my life at that time was Nickolas Muray. I had known him for a very long time, but now I'd fallen in love with him.

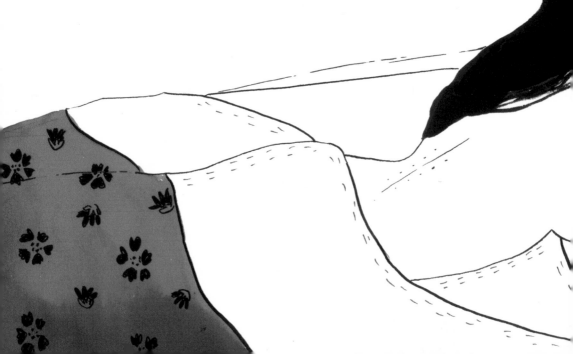

I loved him like no one else. Only Diego had pene-
trated my heart like he had.

From there I flew to Paris because I had been invited by the surrealists to take part in another of their exhibitions. But everything was a disaster from the very beginning. My paintings were retained at customs, and Breton couldn't find a gallery that would show them. Finally, Marcel Duchamp, with whom I'd been staying all that time, organized everything so my work could be exhibited at the Renou et Colle Gallery.

You cannot imagine what bastards those people are. They sit in cafés at all hours, warming their beautiful asses, talking nonstop about culture, art, and revolution and this and that. The next day, they can't eat because none of them work.

Earrings Picasso gave me as a gift.

In general, my stay wasn't pleasant at all. I got sick and the surrealists disappointed me.

I was able to bear those days in Paris because of friends I met, such as Jacqueline Lamba, Mary Reynolds, and Picasso.

The Louvre bought my self-portrait *El marco*, but even though I had an excellent critical reception, I chose not to do a second exhibition.

Paris fashion noticed me, and my bejeweled hand appeared on the cover of *Vogue* magazine. Many years later, so much later that I never saw it, I was on the cover of *Vogue Mexico*, in one of the many beautiful photos for which I posed for Nickolas.

The designer Elsa Schiaparelli even designed a dress called "Madame Rivera."

Still, I wanted to go back to New York.

When I arrived, Nickolas told me he was getting married. He said he felt like he never had a relationship with me, that we were never two, but three, because I always had Diego on my mind. At least he continued to be my friend. I understood, in spite of my profound anguish. I cried for an entire night, then returned to Mexico.

We never stopped being great friends.

I immediately moved back to La Casa Azul. My situation with Diego went from bad to worse. There were rumors he had a relationship with Paulette Goddard and that he wanted to marry her. Around that time he was also accused of attempting to murder Trotsky. Our living arrangement came to an end. We divorced, and he marched off to the United States.

I loved Diego, but I knew our problems would never end. I felt so bad and so alone that I thought no one in the world suffered like I did.

I emptied myself of my tears the same way we had emptied ourselves of our blood.

I drank to drown my sorrows, but those wretches learned to swim.

I had a glazed ceramic clock made with the legend "The hours were broken" and the date "September 1940" because I didn't want to ever forget when we separated.

I cut my hair again because I didn't want to be attractive to Diego. I didn't want to draw attention to any feminine attribute or anything else he could find desirable. I promised myself I would never again depend on a man. I didn't want to see anyone. I worked without pity. I wouldn't stop drinking, and my health suffered for it.

At that difficult moment I became friends with Ramón Mercader. What terrible luck! That demon murdered Trotsky by sinking an icepick into his head. This time, the suspicions fell on me.

My sister Cristina and I were jailed for two days, crying the whole time, until they confirmed we were innocent.

Diego heard about the sorry state of my health, what had happened with Trotsky, and my sadness. He asked me to marry him again, even though it had been less than a year since our separation. Of course I wanted to marry him! But I decided to make him wait while I recovered in San Francisco.

While I was in that city, I had a romance with Heinz Berggruen, a young art collector who fell in love with me at first sight. He came to the hospital to see me every day. As soon as I was better, I moved to New York to spend time with my friends. Heinz went everywhere with me; he didn't hide me. On the one hand, I wanted to go back with Diego; on the other, I enjoyed having fun and living my own life.

I finally went back to Mexico and on December 8, on his fifty-fourth birthday, I married my Diego again.

For the occasion I had the same glazed ceramic clock made, with the same legend, "The hours were broken," but with a new date: "December 1940."

We moved back to La Casa Azul, each of us in our own room. I had one condition: I wouldn't have sex with him any more in order to avoid suffering when he went off with other women, though we didn't always adhere to this rule. I lived there happily with my nieces and nephews, my animals, and the people I loved.

Our marriage was working well. We laughed a lot. I was more understanding and didn't hound him so much about the other women who frequently took up an important part of his heart. I finally learned life was better that way and the rest was just nonsense.

I began to live life to the fullest. I wasn't obsessed with having children anymore. I liked to get dressed up and see the effect it had on people around me. I began to write an autobiography, a diary, which, in the end, became a space of solace.

Who would have thought that stains are alive and help us live.

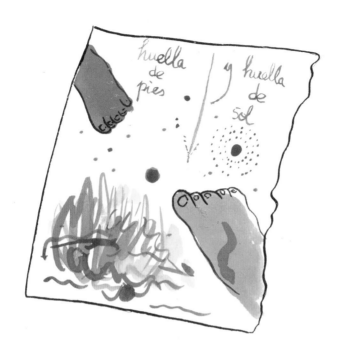

These are some of the photos taken over the course of my life by photographers such as Edward Weston, Héctor García, Imogen Cunningham, Manuel and Lola Álvarez Bravo, Guillermo Zamora, Julien Levy, Nickolas Muray, the Mayo brothers, Juan Guzmán, and Bernice Kolko.

In 1943 I started teaching at the Department of Public Education's School of Painting and Sculpture, which was located down a little street called La Esmeralda.

I would lie on the floor on my belly, and all the students would do the same, and then we'd draw. Whatever you do, don't copy, I'd tell them. Paint your houses, your siblings, the bus, whatever's going on. We played marbles, we played with spinning tops, and I started to become their friend, their very good friend.

I wanted to give them permission to do whatever they wanted, to be themselves, and I tried to elicit a passion for painting in the humblest way I knew.

The first day, I asked them what they wanted to paint, and they asked me to pose for them.

We would usually go out to capture what was happening in the streets, in the city, at the pyramids, so they could understand their past.

Unfortunately, after a few months, my health got so bad that I couldn't go to the school, so I continued the classes at my house. At the beginning, they all came, but over time there were only four left: Fanny Rabel, Arturo García Bustos, Guillermo Monroy, and Arturo "El Gëro." They were known as The Fridos.

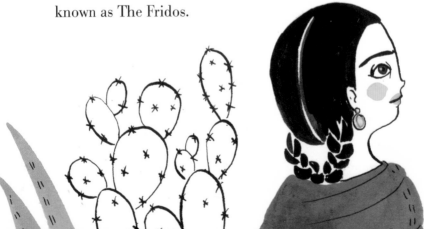

The wounded deer

Then came the return of the pain and fatigue. The doctor recommended a steel corset to help carry the weight of my body, though the pain was ever present. I lost weight, and there were days when my right hand would stiffen. The doctors didn't know what was happening to me. But I couldn't stop painting. I had to be hospitalized several times, at greater expense each time.

If my health were better I could say I was happy, but this sensation that runs from my head to my toe sometimes rattles my brain and makes me bitter.

In 1946, without my sensing it, misfortune arrived. Dr. Philip D. Wilson operated on me in New York. He fused four lumbar vertebrae, did a pelvic graft, and inserted a fifteen-centimeter rod in my back. I went into surgery optimistic, convinced it was for the better, but the pain in the first postoperative weeks was so severe I had to be treated with Demerol and morphine. As a result, I became dependent on them until the last days of my life.

In my weakened state, I was much more vulnerable to Diego's infidelities. The affair he had with the actor María Félix almost drove me to a second divorce.

Diego — beginning
Diego — builder
Diego — my baby
Diego — my boyfriend
Diego — painter
Diego — my lover
Diego — my husband!
Diego — my friend
Diego — my father
Diego — my mother
Diego — my son
Diego — me
Diego — universe
Diversity in unity
Why do I call him My Diego? He never was or
ever will be mine. He is his own.

I was sick for a year (1950—1951). Seven spinal surgeries. Dr. Farill saved me. He helped me recover my joy in living. I'm still in the wheelchair, and I don't know if I'll be able to walk any time soon. I'm still wearing the plaster cast. Although it's a dreadful nuisance, it helps my spine feel better. I'm not in pain.

What I feel is fatigue, and as might be expected, sometimes, desperation. A desperation for which there are no words. But still, I wanted to live. I began to paint the little piece I gave Dr. Farill, which I painted with so much love for him.

The dream

But the reprieve was temporary, and the pain returned. I barely left the house; instead, my friends would come see me. I continued painting, but I stopped making self-portraits and started doing still lifes. I think my work changed because of a combination of brandy, tequila, cognac, and analgesics, or maybe it just happened. There were days when I got my strength back, but for the most part, I would sink into a dark place filled with monsters.

Diego didn't live with me anymore but came to visit constantly. In those moments the room filled with light and tenderness.

My first solo exhibition in Mexico debuted in 1953 at the photographer Lola Álvarez's gallery. The doctor told me I could not leave my bed, so I took it with me to the opening. I drank and sang with all my assistants.

Doc, if you let me drink this tequila, I promise I won't drink at my funeral.

Life went on, and the pain in my right leg got worse until the doctors finally decided to amputate it. And though the pain went away and I was able to walk again, it made me profoundly sad.

Feet, why do I need you, since I have wings to fly!

Diego said if they amputated my leg, they would kill me. He was silent for several days, then he'd mutter nonsense; sometimes he'd cry inconsolably. A part of me was gone forever. I was losing the will to live that had filled everything before.

I'm sorry that soon I'll leave you.

Pain doesn't take permanent residence, and death talked to me in dreams to try to calm me.

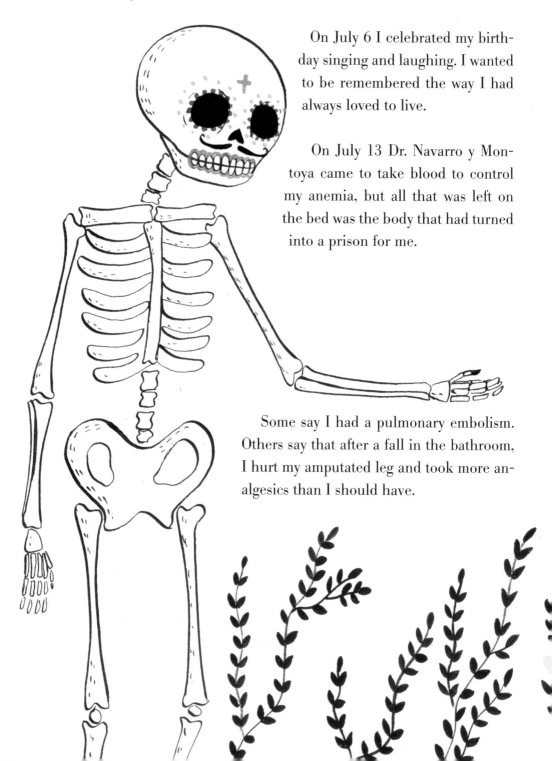

On July 6 I celebrated my birthday singing and laughing. I wanted to be remembered the way I had always loved to live.

On July 13 Dr. Navarro y Montoya came to take blood to control my anemia, but all that was left on the bed was the body that had turned into a prison for me.

Some say I had a pulmonary embolism. Others say that after a fall in the bathroom, I hurt my amputated leg and took more analgesics than I should have.

I hope the exit is joyous, and I hope to never come back.

Interpretation of Her Work: A Chronology

1929. Self-Portrait in Velvet Suit.

A painting she gave to Alejandro Gómez Arias as a gift. On the back there's an inscription that reads: "Now it's forever." She told him the sea in the background was "a symbol of life—my life."

1931. Frida and Diego Rivera.

She painted it two years after her wedding. Frida's feet barely touch the ground, as if she's floating.

Inscription: "Here we are. Me, Frida Kahlo, and my beloved husband, Diego Rivera. I painted these portraits in the beautiful city of San Francisco, California, for our friend Mr. Albert Bender. This was during the month of April in the year 1931."

1932. Henry Ford Hospital.

She painted this after suffering a miscarriage at Henry Ford Hospital. In the draft before the painting, the fetus is absent.

1932. My Birth.

A little after her miscarriage, her mother died.

Right then, she began to make paintings based on Mexican votives. In this painting, the place for the inscription is left blank.

1932. Self-Portrait, Standing at the Border between the United States and Mexico.

Inscription: "Carmen Rivera painted her self-portrait in 1932." Her given name was Magdalena Carmen Frida.

1935. Just a Few Little Cuts.

This painting was inspired by a newspaper article, but it also symbolizes the betrayal by Diego Rivera and her sister Cristina.

1936. My Grandparents, My Parents, and Me.

First family portrait. Her parents appear as they do in their wedding photo. There are theories about the fetus. Some say it's Frida herself. Others say it could be her sister Matilde, with whom her mother was already pregnant when she got married.

1937. Memory.

At a show she had at Julien Levy's in New York; she titled it *Heart*.

1937. Self-Portrait Dedicated to Leon Trotsky.

A birthday gift for Leon Trotsky.
　Inscription: "For Leon Trotsky, I dedicate this painting with all my love, November 7, 1937. Frida Kahlo in San Ángel, Mexico."

1938. The Little Girl Already Has Her Skull Mask.

There is another version of this painting, currently missing.

1939. What the Water Gave Me.

This is what she described to her friend Julien Levy: "It's an image of time passing . . . about time and childhood games in the bathtub and the sadness over what had happened to her over the course of her life."

1939. The Two Fridas.

She painted it as the divorce from Diego Rivera was being finalized. One is the Mexican Frida whom Diego adored, and the other, the more European one, the one Diego abandoned.

In her diary she says the origins of this painting are in an imaginary friend she had as a child.

1940. Altarpiece.

Representation in votive style of the accident she suffered in her adolescence.

1940. The Dream.

Also titled *The Flying Bed*. Life and death are recurrent themes in her work.

1940. Self-Portrait with Thorn Necklace Dedicated to Dr. Eloesser.

Inscription: "I painted my portrait in 1940 for Dr. Leo Eloesser, my doctor and my best friend. With all my love, Frida Kahlo."

1944. The Broken Spine.

The Fridos say that in the original piece she was completely naked. In the end, she covered her pubis because she didn't want to distract from the point about pain that she wanted to make.

1946. The Little Deer.

She gave this painting to Lina and Arcady Boytler, along with this poem: "Here is my portrait, so you'll have me present every day and every night I'm not with you. Every one of my pieces is a study in sadness, but that's my state; I have no repair.

"The little lonesome deer was sad and wounded until she found warmth with Arcady and Lina and felt included."

Reinterpreting Her Work

1939. Dorothy Hale's Suicide.

This illustration is based on that painting. The original features Dorothy Hale and behind her the building from which she jumped.

1946. Tree of Hope.

In the original, she's sitting in front of the stretcher holding the corset. She painted it for the engineer Eduardo Morillo Safa. In her description of it in a letter to him, there's a runaway skeleton as a symbol of life triumphing over death. Later, she eliminated it.

1954. Viva la Vida, Watermelons.

This is said to be last piece she painted. It's true that at the end of her life, she painted many still lifes. Her subject matter may have changed because of her dependence on morphine and Demerol, though there is no way to prove this was the reason for the change.

Bibliography

Books

Colle Corcuera, Marie-Pierre. *Las fiestas de Frida y Diego. Recuerdos y recetas*. Mexico City: Grupo Patria Cultural, 1994. Published in English as *Frida's Fiestas: Recipes and Reminiscences of Life with Frida Kahlo*, by Marie-Pierre Colle Corcuera and Guadalupe Rivera, translated by Kenneth Krabbenhoft and Olga Rigsby (New York: Clarkson Potter, 1994).

Haghenbeck, F. G. *El libro secreto de Frida Kahlo*. Mexico City: Planeta, 2009. Published in English as *The Secret Book of Frida Kahlo*, translation by Achy Obejas (New York: Simon and Schuster, 2012).

Herrera, Hayden. *Frida: Una biografía de Frida Kahlo*. New York: Editorial Diana, 2002. Published in English as *Frida: A Biography of Frida Kahlo* (New York: Harper Perennial, 2002).

Jamis, Rauda. *Frida Kahlo*. Barcelona: Circe, 1988.

Kahlo, Frida. *El diario de Frida Kahlo. Un íntimo autoretrato*. Introduction by Carlos Fuentes. R. M. Verlag. Published in English as *The Diary of Frida Kahlo: An Intimate Self-Portrait* (New York: Abrams, 2005).

Kettenmann, Andrea. *Frida Kahlo, 1907–1954. Dolor y pasión*. Mexico City: Taschen, 2000. Published in English as *Kahlo* (Mexico City: Taschen, 2015).

Zamora, Martha. *Frida. El pincel de la angustia*. Mexico City, 1987. Published in English as *Frida Kahlo: Brush of Anguish*, translation by Marilyn Sode (San Francisco: Chronicle, 1993).

———. *En busca de Frida*. Mexico City, 2015.

Films

A flor de piel. Anecdotes about Frida Kahlo. Department of Culture, FAROS, Mexico City, 2014.

Frida. Directed by Julie Taymor, 2002.

Frida, naturaleza viva. Directed by Paul Leduc. Mexico, 1983.

Frida Kahlo. Documanía, 2012.

Historia de vida–Frida Kahlo. 2014.

Acknowledgments

To Ilustratour, which gave me the opportunity to meet with Lumen and show my work. Thank you for the efforts all these years to create an event by and for illustrators. You'll be missed.

To Xisca Mas, the first to believe in this book; without her this wouldn't have been possible. And Desirée Baudel, who's been incredibly patient while working with me.

To Martha Zamora, who read over my first draft and discovered a Frida I didn't know.

To Alfonso again, for believing in me so completely and giving me confidence in moments when I needed it, for challenging me to do better work and moving me forward. Without him, this book—and everything else—would not have existed.

To Frida, for living her life and leaving us her legacy.

To my mother, the bravest woman I know. My number one fan.